The Adventures of Scuba Jack
Copyright 2021 by Beth Costanzo
All rights reserved

Our seas and oceans have a wide range of fierce creatures. They can look scary, whether it is because of their massive size or their sharp teeth.

But along with these intimidating creatures, there are also sea animals that look funny or humorous. If you were to swim past them in a sea or ocean, you would probably smile, laugh, or want to get closer. These animals are fascinating—not only because of their appearance, but because of the way that they live their lives.

One of those animals is **the pufferfish**. The pufferfish is a fish that is immediately recognizable because of its ability to expand when it feels threatened. But the pufferfish is much more than this. As you will see, the pufferfish is an interesting creature that swims near many of the world's continents.

Some Fascinating Facts About the Pufferfish

The pufferfish has several different names. Technically, it is part of a family called the *Tetraodontidae*. Pufferfish themselves are also called things like puffers, balloonfish, swellfish, toadfish, and the sea squab. While there may be some very slight differences between them, they are often called pufferfish.

Whenever we are talking about the pufferfish, it makes sense to start with its puff-like qualities. Pufferfish look like many other types of fishes when they are safely swimming around. However, when a predator approaches or the pufferfish feels threatened, it starts to change its body. The pufferfish has an extremely elastic stomach, meaning that it can easily expand. When it starts to feel threatened, the pufferfish can fill its stomach with large amounts of water. As this happens, the pufferfish appears much larger. It almost takes on a circular shape, which can be scary and intimidating to larger fish.

The pufferfish's ability to increase in size is known as a defense mechanism. When it feels threatened, it will quickly expand until it feels safer. Along with looking bigger, the pufferfish has pointed spines on its skin. If a predator even wanted to attack the pufferfish when it was bigger, the predator will encounter pointed spines on the pufferfish's skin. Those spines can really hurt, so the predator will probably move on to find other tasty fish to eat.

While the pufferfish has this awesome ability to expand itself when it is scared, its best defense is terrific eyesight. Even though it isn't the best swimmer, it can rely on a quick burst of speed to quickly escape larger fish that want to eat them. All of these defenses do a great job of protecting the pufferfish from other scary animals in the water.

And if an animal does get through these defenses and starts to eat the pufferfish? It will quickly start to feel sick. A large number of pufferfish are toxic, meaning that they are poisonous. Even though the pufferfish may be dead or dying, it can still take down and kill its predator!

Beyond the puffer part of pufferfish, let's talk about some of the less dangerous parts of this creature. Pufferfish are pretty small animals. They can be as small as one inch and can be as large as 24 inches (two feet). Besides seeing pufferfish in an aquarium, you can find them in marine and freshwaters. If you wanted to see them in the wild, you would probably need to go to South America, Africa, or Southeast Asia. Unfortunately, there aren't many pufferfish off of the coasts of the United States, but you may be able to find them near the Chesapeake Bay.

Depending on where they are located, pufferfish tend to eat different things. Most pufferfish eat things like algae and small invertebrate animals. However, some of the larger species can dine on things like clams, mussels, and larger shellfish. If a pufferfish cannot find delicious fish to eat, however, it can survive on vegetation alone.

Like every other animal on our planet, pufferfish have babies. After mating, female pufferfish hatch their eggs after about four days. While the baby pufferfish are extremely tiny, you can see that they start to look like pufferfish—even from their first days of life. Upon birth, they have eyes and mouths and must eat within a few days in order to survive.

Most pufferfish spend their lives in our planet's oceans. However, certain cultures view pufferfish as a delicacy. This means that people from certain countries (like Japan and China) enjoy eating pufferfish, which reduces the number of pufferfish swimming in the wild.

However, when eating pufferfish, humans need to be careful. Like we talked about, pufferfish can be toxic. This means that humans can get sick if the pufferfish isn't properly prepared. There have even been cases where humans have died after eating pufferfish. Unless you have a really good reason for doing it, it is much better to avoid eating pufferfish. Instead, it is much better to observe them from a distance!

Admiring the Pufferfish

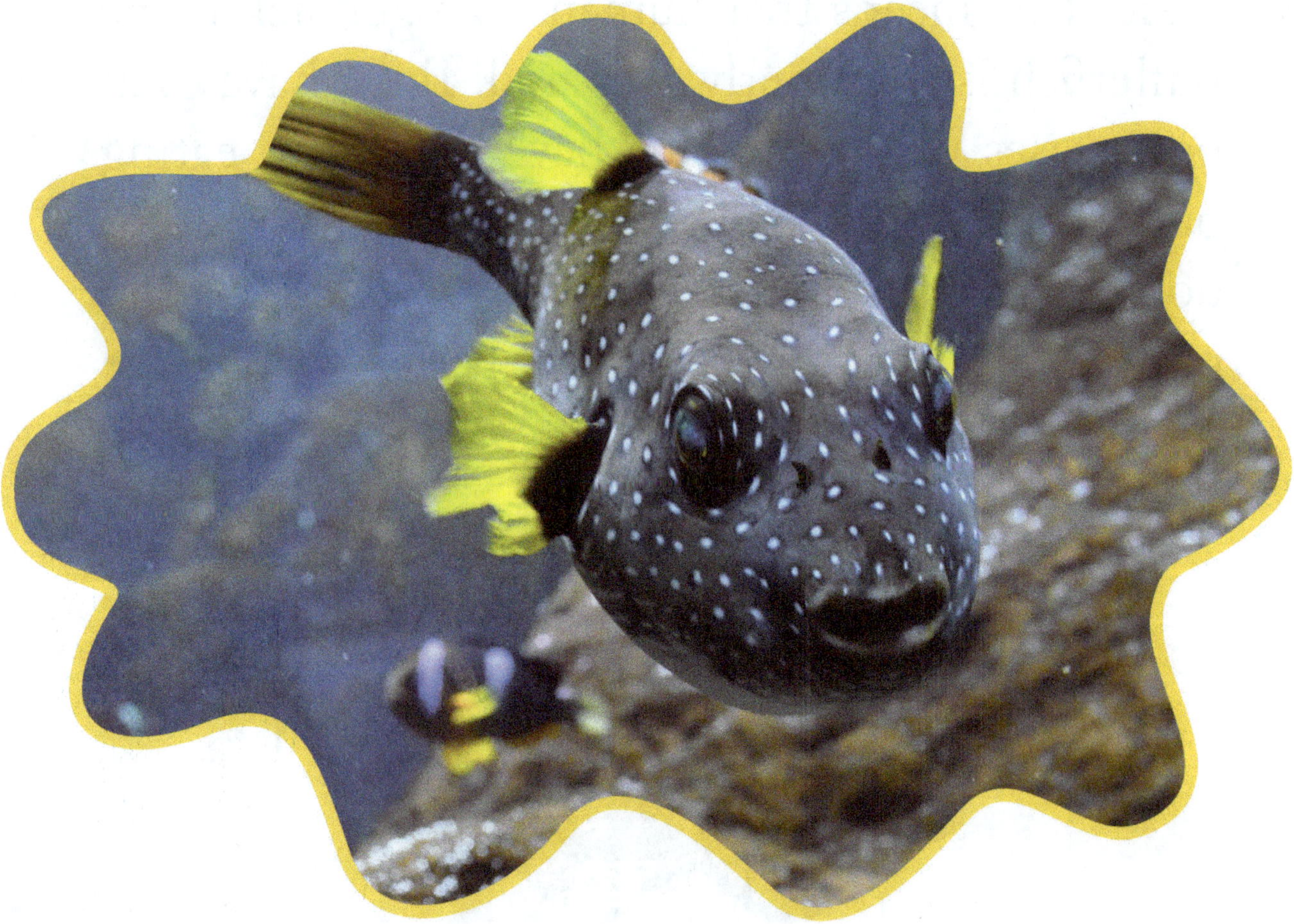

While the pufferfish can look silly, you can see that it can take care of itself in the ocean. Not only does it have many defenses against predators, but it can be an aggressive hunter on its own. Whether you are at the aquarium or see a pufferfish in the wild, I hope that you admire this fascinating creature.

Pufferfish Activities

TRACING

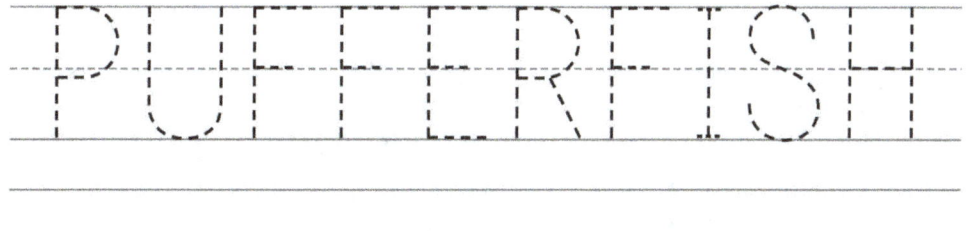

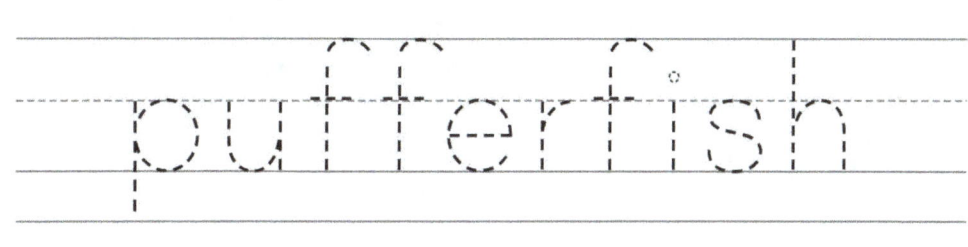

www.adventuresofscubajack.com

COUNTING
Trace the correct answer

7 8 9

8 6 7

10 8 9

10 11 9

www.adventuresofscubajack.com

Dot to Dot
Link the dots then color the result

COLORING

Pufferfish Craft

- Cut the parts below
- Glue the upper part to the body
- Glue the eyes
- Add Dots

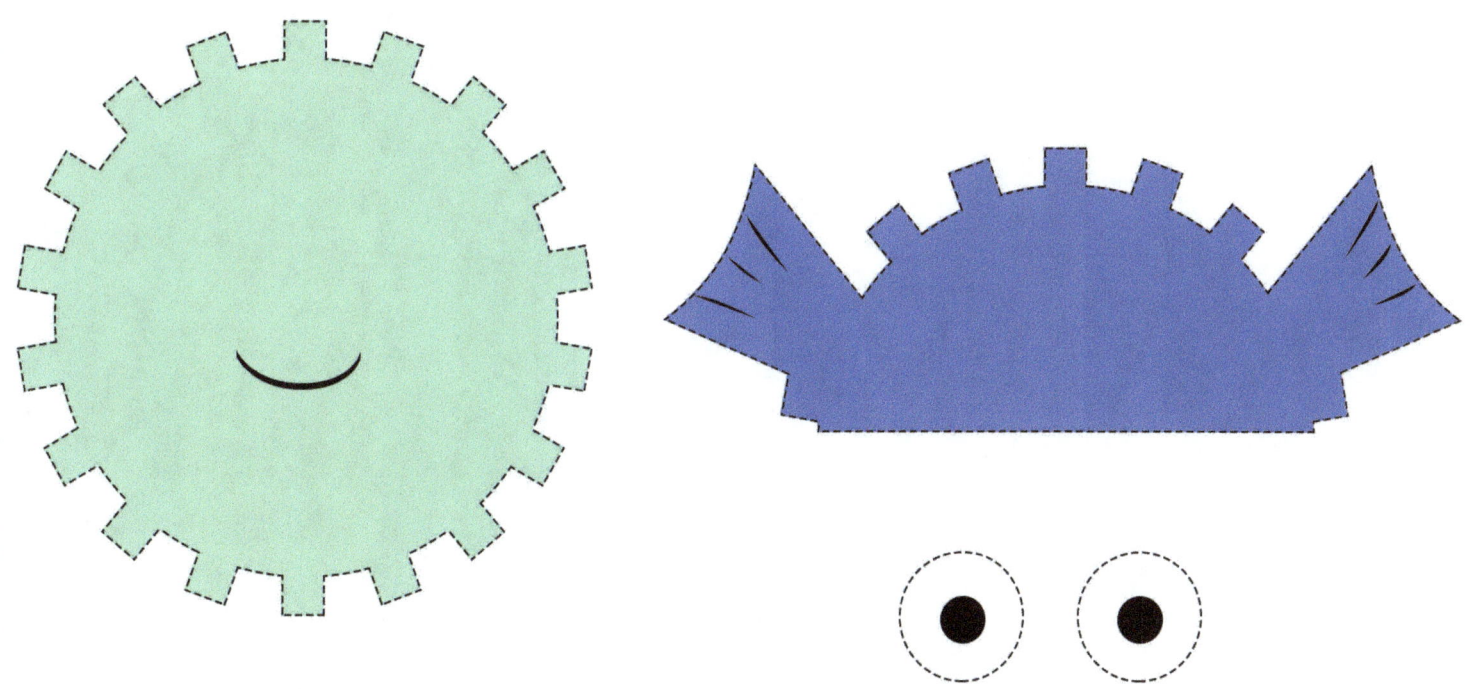

Pufferfish Craft

- Cut the parts below
- Glue the upper part to the body
- Glue the eyes
- Add Dots

Pufferfish Craft

- Cut the parts below
- Glue the upper part to the body
- Glue the eyes
- Add Dots

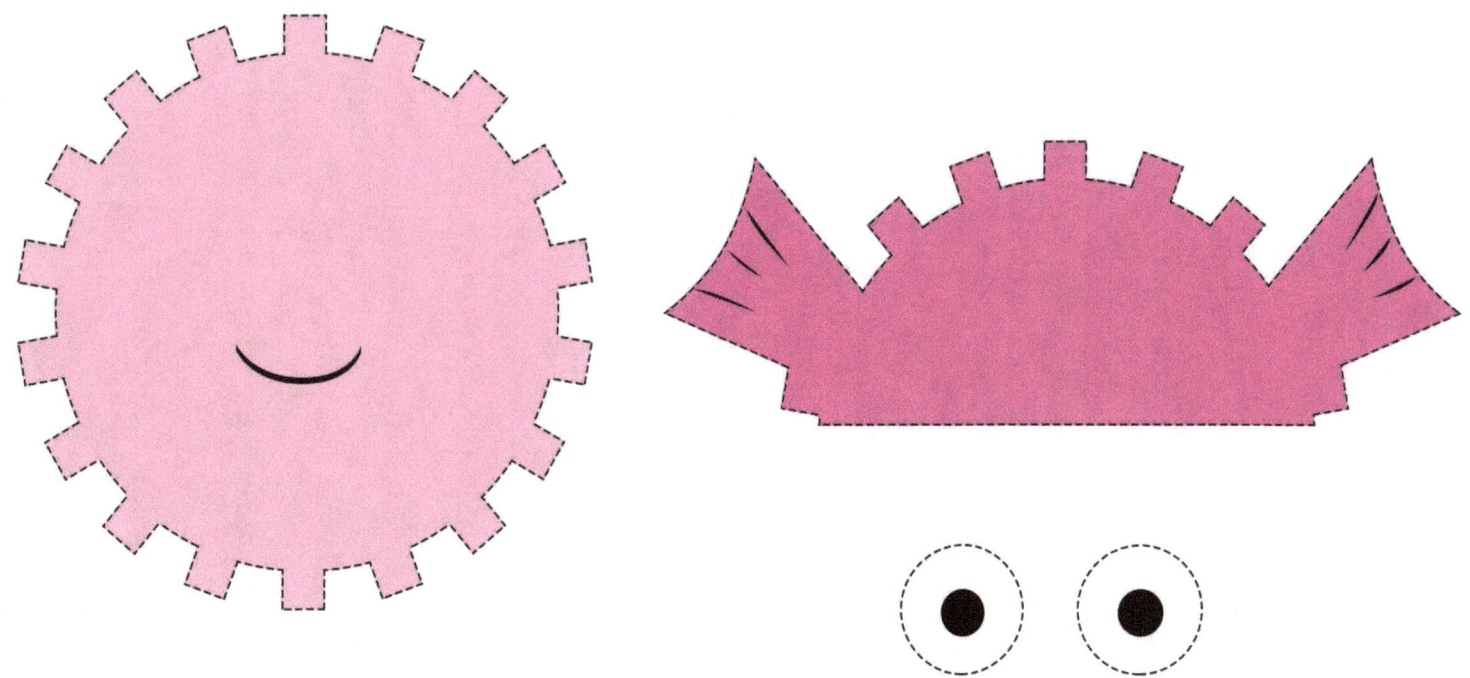

Visit us at:

www.adventuresofscubajack.com

www.ingramcontent.com/pod-product-compliance
Lightning Source LLC
Chambersburg PA
CBHW060429010526
44118CB00017B/2429